JUSTICE

A Bible study by
CHARLES COLSON

D1320100

NAVPRESS ◖◗®
A MINISTRY OF THE NAVIGATORS
P.O. BOX 6000, COLORADO SPRINGS, COLORADO 80934

The Navigators is an international Christian
organization. Jesus Christ gave His followers
the Great Commission to go and make disciples (Matthew 28:19). The aim of The Navigators is to help fulfill that commission by multiply-
ing laborers for Christ in every nation.

NavPress is the publishing ministry of The Navigators. NavPress publications are tools to help
Christians grow. Although publications alone
cannot make disciples or change lives, they
can help believers learn biblical discipleship,
and apply what they learn to their lives and
ministries.

Photography: Mark Reis

Chuck Colson gratefully acknowledges the
researching and writing of Ron Klug in the
preparation of this study guide.

Scripture quotations in this publication are from
the *Holy Bible: New International Version* (NIV).
Copyright © 1973, 1978, 1984, International
Bible Society. Used by permission of Zondervan Bible Publishers. Another version used is
The Living Bible (TLB), copyright 1971 by Tyndale House Publishers, Wheaton, IL. Used by
permission.

Printed in the United States of America

Contents

Author

Charles Colson received his bachelor's degree from Brown University and his law degree from George Washington University. From 1969-1973 he served as special counsel to President Richard M. Nixon. He pleaded guilty to charges related to Watergate in 1974 and served seven months in prison. He is now chairman of Prison Fellowship Ministries, a Washington, D.C.-based organization that he founded in 1976.

Colson is the author of several books, including *Born Again* (Chosen Books, 1976), *Life Sentence* (Chosen Books, 1979), *Loving God* (Zondervan Publishing Co., 1983), *Who Speaks for God?* (Crossway Books, 1985), and *Kingdoms in Conflict* (Morrow/Zondervan Publishing Co., 1987). He is also a frequent contributor to magazines and journals. All of his speaking fees and book royalties are donated to further the work of Prison Fellowship Ministries.

Preface

"Let justice roll on like a river, righteousness like a never-failing stream!" (Amos 5:24). These words of God, spoken through an obscure shepherd named Amos, thundered through Israel 750 years before the birth of Christ. From another prophet, Micah, came a similar injunction: "And what does the LORD require of you? To act justly and to love mercy and to walk humbly with your God" (Micah 6:8).

God's call has not changed over the centuries. Christians today are challenged with this same commandment: to *act justly*.

The world around us is more bereft of God's justice than ever before. The cries of the needy are all around us: from over-crowded prisons, violent inner cities, fractured families, the oppressed powerless, those who live in moral chaos. The only answer to those cries is for God's people to demonstrate His reign—to make His invisible Kingdom visible—by acting justly.

To act justly we must first understand justice from the perspective of God's holy and infallible Word. Justice flows from the character of God Himself. He chose Israel to be His holy nation, a community in which justice was to flow like waters, where those too weak to protect themselves would be treated with dignity and equity.

Sadly, the history of Israel is predominantly a history of failure in that mission. But in God's sovereign plan, Jesus came to announce the Kingdom of God to all who would believe. Jews and Gentiles alike could become citizens of God's holy nation. As members of that Kingdom, we are called to bring His justice and righteousness to bear on the kingdoms of this world.

To act justly we must understand God's holy nature and the sinful nature of man. We must closely examine His biblical injunctions to care for the widows, the poor, the orphans. We are also called to discern a biblical perspective on the deep-rooted social problems so prevalent today.

But more than mere understanding is required. God calls us to be not just hearers, but doers, of His Word. It is time for God's people to emerge from the padded pews of their comfortable churches and enter the arenas of need. For it is there that we can discover how to make God's justice a reality in our society.

And this indeed is our great legacy. For it was activist believers who initiated some of the most magnificent social reforms of recent centuries, founding schools and hospitals, working to abolish slavery, reform prisons, and assert civil rights and human dignity for the oppressed.

The words of God's ancient prophets as well as the commandments of Jesus Himself compel us; the examples of His people who have faithfully pursued justice constrain us. As we learn how to "act justly" in today's desperate and needy culture, may we be found faithful in that holy challenge.

Introduction from the Publisher

"Why does NavPress want to publish a series of Bible studies by Charles Colson?"

This is the question Charles Colson asked of us when we proposed the idea to him.

The answer begins with Jesus' words in Luke 11:28— "Blessed . . . are those who hear the word of God and obey it." Such obedience should result in a vigorous spiritual life which impacts the world around it.

Yet researcher George Barna has made the disturbing observation that Americans who profess a continuing commitment to Jesus Christ evidence few lifestyle differences from non-believers. In terms of surveyable attitudes and behavior patterns—even in such areas as divorce, child abuse, materialism, and civic responsibility—the Body of Christ in the United States looks nearly identical to secular society.

Certainly the problem is not a lack of biblical preaching and teaching. God has raised up many gifted men and women in our time who are regularly bringing His Word to His people through a variety of media.

Perhaps part of the problem is that we are simply not doing what we already know to do. We do not heed Paul's command to the Philippians to put into practice what we learn or receive. Superficial devotion characterizes many segments of American Christianity.

We in NavPress desire to play a strategic part in encouraging the Church toward a vigorous obedience to the Word of God, resulting in a genuine renewal that will strengthen and deepen our impact on society. We believe that we can do this by linking up our resources with the gifted teachers and prophets whom God has raised up in our time—and offering their teaching in a form that will stimulate deeper and more lasting obedience to the Lord Jesus Christ.

We feel that personal Bible study in the context of the Christian small group is an outstanding instrument for this purpose. As a publisher of Bible studies, we are inevitably biased in favor of small groups. However, we have not yet seen a more effective teaching medium through which to generate real change in a person's life. The small group provides accountability, encouragement, fellowship in God's Word, and the power of warm and living spiritual unity, support, and edification so important to the life of the church.

Our strategic aim in this and succeeding studies is to help shape the messages of Charles Colson, whom God has remarkably gifted and empowered for ministry to this generation, into effective tools for small group use. Our desire is that these guides will further deepen and make practical his prophetic and far-reaching call to revolutionary Christian living.

How to Use This Guide

What is the biblical view of justice?
Why should Christians be concerned with issues of justice?
What are the causes of crime?
*What kinds of criteria should we use for evaluating how well
    our prison system works?*
*What is the church's role in reflecting the character of a just
    God?*
How can we reduce the amount of crime in our society?

This study guide is designed to help you seek—and find—
answers to questions like these. It can be used by individuals, but
it will offer the greatest benefits when used in a small group set-
ting, where insights can be shared, questions answered, and differing viewpoints explored. A small group can also help foster
commitment and self-discipline, as members support and
encourage each other in putting biblical teachings into practice.
In a small group Christians can join together in worship and
prayer.

Each session in this study guide is divided into six parts:

1. *Opening Reflection.* Each session begins with an excerpt
from the author's writings. Before you read it, ask the Holy Spirit
to open your mind to His truth. When you come together as a
group, you may want to read it aloud. The questions that imme-
diately follow it, in the "Opening Reflection" section, are to help
you reflect on its meaning and implications. Answer these questions in your personal study, and then discuss them in your
group. Use this discussion as a warm-up for the next part of your
session, which will explore issues arising from key Scripture
passages.

2. *Turning to the Scriptures.* If you are part of a study group,
do your own study first, before the meeting. Allow at least an

11

hour for this preparation. Some of the questions ask you to look at what the Bible *says*. Others direct you to think about what the Bible *means*. Still others encourage you to *apply* the Scriptures to your own life and the life of your community.

When you come together as a group, discuss your answers. Come with the intention of learning from one another. The proper attitude is one of humility before God's Word and one another.

Some of the issues discussed in this study—for example, capital punishment—are emotionally charged for many people. Remember that in a Christian group, you are gathering as brothers and sisters in Christ, seeking His lordship. Encourage the expression of differing viewpoints. Always come back to the question, "What is God saying to us through His Word?"

It will probably be helpful to designate a leader to guide the discussion. If the group begins to get too far off the track, the leader can gently bring it back to the Bible study or the issues at hand.

3. *For Further Reflection.* Following the Bible study are some quotations from Charles Colson and other Christian writers. Use these excerpts as springboards for your thinking and discussion. In your private study, read them slowly and thoughtfully, jotting down any questions or thoughts you have. Share these notes in your group meetings.

4. *Moving into Action.* "Do not merely listen to the word, and so deceive yourselves. Do what it says," wrote the Apostle James (James 1:22). And Jesus gave us His promise: "Everyone who hears these words of mine and puts them into practice is like a wise man who built his house on the rock" (Matthew 7:24).

After reflecting on the Bible and selected Christian writings, we move into action, putting God's Word into practice and deepening our learning. These actions can then lead to further reflection.

It is important that you as an individual and as a group take at least some of these actions. However, don't feel that you have to do them all. Group members can choose from among the activities, working as individuals, in pairs, or as a subgroup. Some activities would be appropriate for the whole group.

Schedule time for these activities between your group meetings. When you meet as a group, share what you did and your reactions to it. This will provide an excellent opportunity for you to learn from one another.

5. *Ideas for Group Worship.* Conclude your group meeting with worship. (You may also wish to end your personal study with prayer and praise.) Worship gives glory to God and helps establish group unity and harmony by creating a common focus on the Lord. Communal prayer and worship can reduce or even eliminate any tensions which have built up in the group.

Feel free to adapt the worship suggestions to your particular group. You may, for example, want to do more singing. Perhaps one person in the group could serve as worship leader, or leadership could be rotated.

6. *Reading Resources.* Optional resources are suggested at the end of each session for those who wish to dig more deeply into a topic.

The Justice of God

" This is indeed the very heart of the relationship God demands with His people, expressed in the covenant: "I am the Lord your God; consecrate yourselves and *be holy because I am holy.*" Understanding this basic covenant, the character of God, and what He expects is essential to understanding the New Covenant. For the character of God has not changed, nor has His expectation of holiness from His people.

In fact, the same remarkable promise that God made to Moses—that He would *pitch* His *tent* and dwell in the midst of His people—is a central theme throughout Scripture. In the familiar passage of John's gospel, "The Word became flesh, and *dwelt* among us," the Greek word for *dwelt* literally means to "pitch a tent." So now, through Christ, God comes to "pitch His tent" among His people. And to carry the theme to its conclusion, John, in describing his apocalyptic vision of the new heaven and new earth, writes, "The tabernacle of God is among men, and He shall dwell among them, and they shall be His people." Again the word *dwell* is literally translated to "pitch a tent."

Thus, from Exodus to Revelation we find the identical imagery, a holy God "pitching His tent" among His people: first in the tabernacle, then in Christ and Christ in us, and ultimately in His kingdom.

Salvation, therefore, is not simply a matter of being separated from our past and freed from our bondage to sin; salvation means also that we are joined to a holy God. By pitching His tent in our midst, God identifies with His people through His very presence. The reality of a "God who is here"—personal and in our midst—is an extraordinary assurance, one which distinguishes the Judeo-Christian faith from all other religions.

15

But God demands something in return for His presence. He demands that we identify with Him—that we be holy because He is holy.

Holiness is not an option. God will not tolerate our indifference to His central command. It is the central covenant and command of Scripture, the "cardinal point on which the whole of Christianity turns," William Wilberforce wrote. It is not just for well-known saints like Mother Teresa, but for every believer.

What does this mean for us, then, in the real world in which we live every day?

Loving God

Opening Reflection

1. Why do you think it is important for us to understand the holiness of God?

2. Reflect on the imagery the Bible uses to portray God's relationship with His people—God "pitching His tent" among His people. What are the implications of this truth for how we ought to live? (Draw on the excerpt above, your own thoughts, or relevant scripture passages for your answer.)

Turning to the Scriptures

3.   a. What are we to "boast about" or "glory in," according to Jeremiah 9:23-24?

b. What are we especially to understand about God?

4. Through the prophet Jeremiah, God spoke to Shallum, a corrupt king of Judah, about his father Josiah, one of Judah's just kings (see Jeremiah 22:11-17, particularly verses 15-16).

a. What did Josiah do that pleased God?

b. What did Josiah's actions reveal about his relationship to God (verse 16)?

c. What does this passage teach about the relationship between knowing God and acting justly?

Note: The Hebrew word for "justice" is a word rich in meanings. It is sometimes translated "righteousness" or "holiness."

5. Read Psalm 146:5-10, noting especially the verbs that express God's actions.

a. List the actions here.

b. What can we know of God's nature and character based upon what this passage reveals about Him?

c. How might God be carrying out each of these works today?

6. All of the following passages proclaim the justice of God, yet each does so in a different context.

a. For each passage, identify the distinct dimension of God's character that is coupled with His justice.

Psalm 9:7-8

Psalm 33:5

Isaiah 30:18

b. What do you think would be one practical outcome if what you learn of God in these passages were truly to take hold in your life?

7. How can Deuteronomy 32:3-4 help us understand what the Bible means when it says that God is "just"?

8.   a. Who are the recipients of God's justice in the following passages?

Deuteronomy 10:17-18

Psalm 35:10

Psalm 103:6

Psalm 140:12

b. Why do you think Scripture singles out people in these circumstances as those in need of God's justice?

9. Matthew 12:15-21 proclaims Jesus' fulfillment of the prophecy in Isaiah 42:1-4.

a. Summarize the predictions made about Jesus in this prophecy.

b. From your knowledge of Jesus' life and ministry, how did He reveal the character of God in seeking justice?

10. Read carefully Romans 3:21-26.

a. What do you learn here about how God's justice is carried out?

b. How do you think this demonstration of God's justice should shape the way we respond to God and to our fellow human beings?

11. a. What does the psalmist sing about God in Psalm 101:1?

b. Which of these statements do you think most clearly expresses the biblical picture of God?

- God is loving in spite of His being just.

- God is just because He is loving.

12. Read 2 Thessalonians 1:6-10 and Revelation 19:1-16 and 21:1-8.

a. When will the justice of God be fully accomplished?

b. What is the ultimate outcome of God's justice?

13. Has this study enlarged or changed your understanding of God in any way? If so, how?

14. Take a few minutes to list any questions you have after working through this first chapter. The quotations in the following section, "For Further Reflection," may throw some light on your questions. You might also find answers in some of the resources listed in the bibliography at the end of this chapter. Bring any remaining questions to your next group session, or ask for help from a friend or trusted acquaintance.

For Further Reflection
Meditate on the following statements in light of the Bible study you have just done. Write down any thoughts or questions you may have. If you are part of a study group, share your reflections in the group.

The word justice *in the Bible refers to conformity to a rule or norm. God plays by the rules. The ultimate norm of justice is His own holy character. . . . What God does is always consistent with who God is.*

R. C. Sproul,
The Holiness of God

The biblical concept of justice is much different and even more foreign to modern Americans. Far from being impartial, it reflects special concern for protecting vulnerable people from victimization by the powerful. Justice is so closely linked with the concepts of righteousness and peace that the three often merge. It brings judgment on the wrongdoer but also works to restore the victim, the offender and the community. And most important, it stems not from the image of a minor Greek goddess [Justicia], but from the character of the one true God, Jehovah.

Daniel W. Van Ness,
Crime and Its Victims

A simpler and more familiar solution for the problem of how God can be just and still justify the unjust is found in the Christian doctrine of redemption. It is that, through the work of Christ in atonement, justice is not violated but satisfied when God spares a sinner. Redemptive theology teaches that mercy does not become effective toward a man until justice has done its work. The just penalty for the sin was exacted when Christ our Substitute died for us on the cross. However unpleasant this may sound to the ear of the natural man, it has ever been sweet to the ear of faith. Millions have been morally and spiritually transformed by this message, have lived lives of great moral power, and died at last peacefully trusting in it.

A. W. Tozer,
The Knowledge of the Holy

[The] call to a holy life is based on the fact that God Himself is holy. Because God is holy, He requires that we be holy. Many Christians have what we might call a "cultural holiness." They adapt to the character and behavior pattern of Christians around them. As the Christian culture around them is more or less holy, so these Christians are more or less holy. But God has not called us to be like those around us. He has called us to be like Himself. Holiness is nothing less than conformity to the character of God.

Jerry Bridges,
The Pursuit of Holiness

Christ tells us we must lose our life for His sake in order to find it. We discover meaning and purpose not in the search for self, but in surrender of self, in obedience to Christ. In right relationship with our Creator, knowing we belong to Him, we pour ourselves out in service to others.

Charles Colson,
Who Speaks for God?

Moving into Action

Now is the time to begin putting into action what you have learned. This important step will help you continue and deepen your learning. If you are part of a group, divide up the action steps in this and the following sessions. You can work as individuals, in pairs, or in small groups. Be prepared to report back to the whole group at your next meeting.

1. Learn more about the biblical concept of justice by doing a word study. Use Bible dictionaries such as the following:

Tyndale House Publishers, *The Illustrated Bible Dictionary* (Wheaton, Ill.: Tyndale House Publishers, 1980).
G. W. Bromiley, ed. *The International Bible Encyclopedia* (Grand Rapids: Eerdmans Publishing Co., 1982).
Paul J. Achtemeier, ed. *Harper's Bible Dictionary* (San Francisco: Harper & Row, 1985).

2. Report on the work of Justice Fellowship, P.O. Box 17181, Washington, DC 20041-0180, (703) 834-3650. Suggest ways that Christians can share in this work.

3. Begin a file of articles from current newspapers and magazines on issues of justice, crime, the court system, prisons, and alternatives to imprisonment. Continue to add to it throughout this study. All members of your group may want to share in this activity.

4. Read Charles Colson's autobiography, *Born Again,* and give a brief summary to your group.

Ideas for Group Worship

Read aloud Psalm 33. One person may read it, while others reflect silently; you may all read it together; or you may read it antiphonally, with a leader reading the first half of each verse and the others responding with the second half. Close by asking God to help you understand His justice. Ask the Holy Spirit to make your study take root and to prompt the action steps you will be taking.

Reading Resources

Jerry Bridges, *The Pursuit of Holiness* (Colorado Springs, Colo.: NavPress, 1978), esp. "The Holiness of God."

Charles Colson, *Born Again* (Old Tappan, N.J.: Fleming H. Revell, 1976).

J. I. Packer, *Knowing God* (Downers Grove, Ill.: InterVarsity Press, 1973), esp. "God the Judge."

R. C. Sproul, *The Holiness of God* (Wheaton, Ill.: Tyndale House Publishers, 1985), esp. "Holy Justice."

Daniel W. Van Ness, *Crime and Its Victims* (Downers Grove, Ill.: InterVarsity Press, 1986), esp. "Justice and Righteousness."

The Holy Nation

At the height of the energy crisis in 1977, the governor of Virginia ordered energy use restricted in non-essential buildings. No one seemed particularly surprised that churches headed his list. In the eyes of the world, as well as many church-goers, the church is only a building, and an expensive, under-used one at that; except for a few hours on Sunday and an occasional mid-week service or function, the building sits empty. So why use scarce resources to heat it?

These same people consider the church just another institution with its own bureaucracy, run by ministers and priests who, like lawyers and doctors, are members of a profession (though not so well-paid). And while this parochial institution fulfills a worthwhile social and inspirational function, rather like an arts society or civic club, most people could get along fine without it.

In many ways, of course, the church has allowed itself to become what the world says it is. (This seems to be a common human bent—to become what others consider us to be.) But that sad fact has not dulled or changed God's definition of, and intention for, His church. For biblically the church is an *organism,* not an organization—a *movement,* not a monument. It is not a part of the community; it is a whole new community. It is not an orderly gathering; it is a new order with new values, often in sharp conflict with the values of the surrounding society.

The church does not draw people in; it sends them out. It does not settle into a comfortable niche, taking its place alongside the Rotary, the Elks, and the country club. Rather, the church is to make society uncomfortable. Like yeast, it unsettles the mass around it, changing it from within. Like salt, it flavors and preserves that into which it vanishes.

But as yeast is made up of many particles and salt composed of multiplied grains, so the church is many individual believers. For God has given us each other; we do not live the Christian life alone. We do not love God alone.

To believe Jesus means we follow Him and join what He called the "kingdom of God" which He said was "at hand." This is a "new commitment . . . a new companionship, a new community established by conversion."

Consider how Aristides described the Christians to the Roman Emperor Hadrian:

> They love one another. They never fail to help widows; they save orphans from those who would hurt them. If they have something they give freely to the man who has nothing; if they see a stranger, they take him home, and are happy, as though he were a real brother. They don't consider themselves brothers in the usual sense, but brothers instead through the Spirit, in God.

Aristides was describing the kingdom of God made visible by believers.

Loving God

Opening Reflection
1. What is your understanding of the church?

2. In what ways can believers today "make visible" the Kingdom of God?

3. In what contexts have you most clearly experienced God's Kingdom?

Turning to the Scriptures

4.   a. Read Exodus 19:3-6. When God led the people of Israel from Egypt and gave them His Law on Mount Sinai, what special role did He give them? (Compare Deuteronomy 7:6.)

   b. How were the people to carry out this role?

   c. According to verse 4, what was to be their motive for doing this?

5. God's intention was that Israel should be a *shalom* community, one in which God's people lived in peace and unity and justice. To help them understand what that meant, God gave them His Law, which we find in Old Testament books such as Exodus, Leviticus, Numbers, and Deuteronomy. How does each of the following passages describe what their community life was to be like?

Deuteronomy 10:12-22

Deuteronomy 16:18-20

Deuteronomy 24:17-18

6. When Israel failed to "make the invisible kingdom visible," God sent His prophets, such as Amos, to remind them of their role as God's special people. In what ways had Israel failed to be a holy nation?

Amos 4:1

Amos 5:7

Amos 5:11-12

7. Through the prophets God also promised a Messiah who would establish God's "holy nation." Compare Isaiah 61:1-4 with Luke 4:16-21.

    a. What did Jesus come to do that would show He was God's Messiah?

    b. In what sense was Jesus establishing God's holy nation?

8.   a. What does Peter call the New Testament believers in 1 Peter 2:9-10?

    b. What does this passage suggest about the relationship between Old Testament Israel and the New Testament church?

9. a. What do you learn about the New Testament believers in Revelation 5:9-10?

b. In what sense is the worldwide church (all Christians everywhere) a holy nation?

10. Is it possible for a political nation, such as the United States, to be, or be patterned after, God's "holy nation"? Why or why not?

11. What do you think is the individual Christian's role as a member of God's holy nation, the church?

12. Many Christians are unaware of how they are making God's Kingdom—for example, in performing a simple act of kindness for a neighbor.

What are some of the ways that you are already making "the invisible Kingdom visible" . . .

in your family?

in your work?

in your neighborhood?

in your country?

in the world?

13. List any questions here that have come up in your study so far.

For Further Reflection

Peter understood that the "holy nation" was not just another description of the church, but a real nation instituted and bound together by the Holy Creator of heaven and earth, at whose sovereign pleasure all the kingdoms of man are allowed to exist. To understand that we are members of the holy nation should evoke our deepest reverence.

But we live in an age in which the church seems to be beating a steady retreat in the face of the advancing forces of secular culture. And if we are honest, we must admit there's more of the world in the church than there is the church in the world.

Charles Colson,
Dare to Be Different, Dare to Be Christian

The gospel in the New Testament in addition to offering everlasting life also aims at restoring the quality of life God intended us to have here and now. It includes a strong emphasis upon the development of God's people who are called to be a model community in the world as witness to God's grace in their communal existence.

Clark Pinnock,
A Case for Faith

The insistence that the church is a "nation" is one that also has profound political implications. It is a way of saying that no other institution or regime can claim our absolute loyalties. If the church is a holy nation of which we are citizens, we must be very careful about what we offer to the other "nations" in which we find ourselves. Our Christian citizenship must always be foremost in our minds; it must be our point of reference when the claims of other "citizenships" are thrust upon us.

Richard J. Mouw,
Called to Holy Worldliness

The church's transcendent vision holds the world accountable to something beyond itself. In doing so, its members serve as ambassadors, citizens of the heavenly Kingdom at work in this world.

Charles Colson,
Kingdoms in Conflict

Holy living isn't just personal piety; it is standing for justice and righteousness in society. We can't pay someone else to do that; we don't get off the hook by tithing or paying dues to some moralistic organization. God calls each one of us to live it out ourselves. That can be painful and bloody; usually it means getting our hands dirty. Always there is a cost.

Charles Colson,
The Struggle for Men's Hearts and Minds

Moving into Action

Have group members report on the action steps they have taken since your last meeting. If someone has brought newspaper or magazine clippings, ask him or her to summarize them briefly. You might want to set them out on a table so others can review them after the session.

1. Read *Dare to Be Different, Dare to Be Christian* by Charles Colson (Wheaton, Ill.: Victor, 1986). Look for insights on how the church is to be a distinctively new community within society.

2. Report on the work of one Christian, William Wilberforce, to outlaw slavery in England. Suggested resources: chapter eight of Charles Colson's book *Kingdoms in Conflict* (Grand Rapids: Zondervan, 1987); Garth Lean's biography of Wilberforce, *God's Politician* (Colorado Springs, Colo.: Helmers & Howard, 1987; foreword by Charles Colson), which traces Wilberforce's strategy for changing his times.

3. Continue to look for current articles on justice issues.

Ideas for Group Worship

Sing together a hymn like "O Worship the King" or "Crown Him with Many Crowns." (If your group is not comfortable singing together, try reading the hymn aloud.) Consider having a time of prayer and praise in which you focus on Christ as Lord and King.

Reading Resources

Charles Colson, *Dare to Be Different, Dare to Be Christian* (Wheaton, Ill.: Victor Books/Scripture Press, 1986).

Charles Colson, *Kingdoms in Conflict* (Grand Rapids: Zondervan, 1987), esp. "Politics of the Kingdom."

Charles Colson, *Loving God* (Grand Rapids: Zondervan Publishing Co., 1983), esp. "The Holy Nation."

Richard Mouw, *Called to Holy Worldliness* (Philadelphia: Fortress Press, 1980), esp. "The People of God in the World."

Defending the Defenseless

The crowd seemed intent as I traced the history of Prison Fellowship. They laughed when I told them of neighbors around Fellowship House confusing congressmen and convicts; there was scattered applause once or twice when I talked about our vision of bringing men and women out of prison into training sessions.

The heat in the room was overpowering. By now every stitch of clothing on my body was wet through; I'm sure I looked like I'd just come in from the rain. This should have brought weakness but instead came strength. Words and sentences I'd never said before flowed out of me, as if they were raised up from the inner recesses of my spirit. I talked on about my own decision to go into prison work full-time, about the amazing love that Jesus has for those of us who have fallen.

"Jesus Christ came into this world for the poor, the sick, the hungry, the homeless, the imprisoned. He is the Prophet of the loser. And all of us assembled here are losers. I am a loser just like every one of you. The miracle is that God's message is specifically for those of us who have failed.

"Jesus rode into Jerusalem on a donkey," I said at the end. "He did this so that people would know that He came from the dirt and the mud, that He had been with weak and ordinary people and those who hurt and suffered.

"The message of Jesus Christ is for the imprisoned—for your families, some of them who aren't making it on welfare on the outside. Christ reached out for you who are in prison because He came to take those chains off, to take you out of bondage. He can make you the freest person in the entire world, right here in this lousy place.

"Jesus, the Savior, the Messiah, the Jesus Christ I follow

37

is the One who comes to help the downtrodden and the oppressed and to release them and set them free. This is the Jesus Christ to whom I have committed my life. This is the Jesus Christ to whom I have offered up my dream and said, 'Lord, I want to help these men because I have lived among them. I came to know them, I love them. There is injustice in our society, but we can change it. Yes, God, we can change it. I give my life to it.'"

What happened next can only be explained as an extraordinary outpouring of the Holy Spirit. Men were not only standing throughout the auditorium, they were getting up on their chairs, clapping and shouting. The change in the faces was awesome. They were warm and smiling. There were tears in the eyes of many where before there had been distrust and hate. It was the ultimate for me in learning how to be used of God; I was the wheel—He the Potter.

Life Sentence

Opening Reflection

1. How would you have felt if you had been present at this encounter with prisoners at the Atlanta Penitentiary?

2. Why do you think the prisoners responded as they did?

3. "Jesus Christ is the Prophet of the loser."

   a. How is that true for those in prison?

   b. How is that true for those outside?

4. Have you found this statement to be true in your life? Why or why not?

Turning to the Scriptures
5. Read Isaiah 1:11-17 and 58:1-14.

   a. What was God criticizing in the religious life of His people?

b. What did God expect of His people that they were failing
to do?

c. In your opinion what message does this prophecy have for
contemporary believers?

6.   a. For what did Jesus criticize the scribes and Pharisees in
Matthew 23:23?

b. How would you apply His words to believers today?

7.   a. Who are identified as likely victims of injustice in each of
the following passages?

Exodus 23:6

Jeremiah 22:3

Ezekiel 22:29

Amos 5:12

b. Compare this list with our society today. Which individuals or groups do you think have the most difficult time receiving justice?

8. Read Amos 5:24. What would life be like in a community that lived up to this command?

9. a. What characteristic of justice is emphasized in Leviticus 19:15?

b. How should this characteristic be applied to the likely victims of injustice identified in question 7 of this chapter?

10. a. What does God command in Amos 5:15?

b. How might ordinary Christians today carry out this command? Be as specific as you can.

11. a. What victims of injustice are named in Jeremiah 21:12 and 22:3?

b. What does God encourage us to do for them?

12. a. Read Luke 10:25-37. What did the good Samaritan do to help a victim of crime?

b. In today's society, who is your "neighbor"?

c. In what ways might you be able to help a victim of crime?

13. a. What kind of injustice is spoken of in the following passages?

Job 31:13-14

Jeremiah 22:13

James 5:1-4

b. What are the implications of these passages for conditions that you are aware of in your community, or in society at large?

14. Summarize what you have learned so far by completing this sentence: "Justice is . . ."

15. a. What do you feel is the biggest barrier to your doing more to "seek justice"?

b. What might help you overcome this barrier?

16. List any questions you may have at this point in your study.

For Further Reflection

Jesus went on to demonstrate in His ministry a deep compassion for the suffering and the forgotten. He fed the hungry, healed the lame, gave sight to the blind. He was concerned not only with saving man from hell in the next world but delivering him from the hellishness of this one. Thus, the Son reflected the Father's passion for mercy and justice. And His message of social justice was just as unsettling and convicting as it was in the time of Amos—and as it is today.

Charles Colson,
Loving God

In biblical justice, the openness of Christian love to the unlovely is a principle of behavior cutting across the distinctions of society. In its combination of the affirmation of the equal worth of each person in the community with sensitivity to the needs of each person or group, biblical justice is most concerned with those who are on the fringes of the community. It is dynamic justice which can create a free nation out of slaves.

Stephen Charles Mott,
Biblical Ethics and Social Change

We share the Good News, feed the hungry, visit the imprisoned, seek justice for the oppressed and care for the widows and orphans, not because we are do-gooders or taken in by the social gospel, but out of appreciation for what God has done in our lives. When Christians by the millions practice this kind of obedience in all walks of life, we will see the culture profoundly impacted; for the strongholds of Satan cannot stand against this kind of holy power.

Charles Colson,
Who Speaks for God?

Moving into Action

Begin by having group members report on the action steps they have taken. If anyone has brought articles on justice issues, take time to share them briefly.

Let group members choose from among these action steps. Don't feel that you have to do all of them.

1. Do some study into the historical background of Israel's likely victims of injustice (question 7a of this chapter). What were conditions like for them? Why are they repeatedly singled out for concern?

2. Find out what help is available to victims of crime in your community or your state.

3. Visit a courtroom while court is in session. Report back to your group on what you have observed.

4. If you have served on a jury, report on your experience.

5. Learn about the kind of legal aid available to poor people in your community.

6. Interview a lawyer or judge to learn what you can about their perspective on justice issues in your community.

7. Continue to look for articles on justice issues, such as the court systems, the death penalty, and the punishment of offenders.

Ideas for Group Worship

Gather in a circle for prayer. Let each member who feels moved to do so pray a brief prayer for some aspect of justice. Include prayers for the victims of crime and injustice, for judges and lawyers, for law enforcement officers, for others you know who are working for justice. Pray about the action steps you will be taking. Ask God to show you any other ways you might act on behalf of justice.

Reading Resources

Charles Colson, *Loving God* (Grand Rapids: Zondervan Publishing Co., 1983), esp. pages 183-197.

Stephen Charles Mott, *Biblical Ethics and Social Change* (New York: Oxford University Press, 1982), esp. "God's Justice and Ours."

Daniel W. Van Ness, *Crime and Its Victims* (Downers Grove, Ill.: InterVarsity Press, 1986), esp. pages 113-125.

Crime and Punishment

"Since one out of three American households will be affected by crime this year, there are increasing numbers of victims who angrily—and rightly—demand justice.

I understand how they feel. Six years ago our home was burglarized. Among the valuables stolen were White House memorabilia, my college ring and sterling silver pieces my grandfather had made. They were irreplaceable. Patty and I were outraged over losing family relics and, even more, over having the privacy of our home invaded. Ironically, I was out of town visiting a prison the day the burglary took place.

Then, just a year ago, a young man snatched my briefcase in the Miami airport while my back was turned. The briefcase could be replaced, but not the hundreds of speech notes that were in it.

Both times I experienced the full fury of unvented anger. Had I been able to catch the young man in the airport, I might have momentarily forsaken my Christian witness and wrestled him to the ground.

This mixture of fear and fury is a natural—and valid— reaction. But though it is understandable, the very emotionalism of the issue is what threatens hope for a rational solution. Already we are being dangerously polarized. So-called law and order advocates see those of us who want reform as "soft" on crime, as being against punishment.

But this is not the issue. Christians, in particular, understand the need for punishment. Ours is a God of justice who exacts punishment for sin. When Adam and Eve disobeyed His first commandment, God pronounced the sentence all mankind lives under to this day. His wrath is swift and sure, as the Israelites learned when they cajoled Aaron into making the idolatrous golden calf, and as Ananias and Sapphira discovered in the early days of the Christian church.

Despite modern psychologists who argue that societal conditions like poverty cause crime, the Judeo-Christian view sees man as responsible for his own moral choices. Throughout the ordinances given to Moses at Mt. Sinai is the consistent theme of individual accountability. Man is held to account under the threat of punishment for the consequences of his actions.

The biblical rationale for government, in fact, is to preserve order and to restrain man from inflicting his sin upon others. The first example of this was God's stationing the angel with the flaming sword in the Garden of Eden to protect the tree of knowledge. So we Christians are commanded in the much discussed verses of Romans 13 to obey and submit to governing authorities. God has ordained that order be maintained. Government, with its power to protect and punish, is His instrument.

The issue, then, is not *whether* society is to punish, but *how* it is to punish.

Who Speaks for God?

Opening Reflection

1. Have you ever been the victim of crime? How did the crime make you feel toward the offender?

2. Go back to the statement above that "Ours is a God of justice who exacts punishment for sin." What is your understanding of how God punishes sin?

3.   a. Do you agree that an important role of government is to punish wrongdoing? Why or why not?

b. What do you think should be society's purpose in punishing those who break its laws?

Turning to the Scriptures

4. Read Mark 7:1-23, in which Jesus responds to the Pharisees' criticism of Him and the disciples for neglecting ceremonial washing.

a. According to verses 21-23, where does crime have its origins?

b. What role do you think societal conditions—such as poverty, racism, violence on TV, divorce—play in the increase of crime?

5.   a. What does each of these passages reveal about God's attitude when He punishes?

Psalm 89:30-33

Psalm 99:8

Ezekiel 33:11

b. How do you think we should reflect God's character in our attitudes toward those in our families or communities who are to be punished?

6.   a. Read Romans 12:17-21, in which Paul discusses the Christian's response to those who do wrong to us. Summarize briefly Paul's instructions.

b. In verse 20, Paul quotes from Proverbs 25:21-22. Commentators believe that this image of heaping burning coals on the enemy's head may refer back to an Egyptian ritual in which carrying a basin of glowing coals on one's head signified the individual's repentance.

Paul's sense, therefore, is that to do good to one's enemy may bring about his repentance.

In what ways do you think Paul's teaching in this passage should impact how we treat those who are being punished?

7. In Romans 7:7-20 Paul discusses some weighty issues regarding the struggle with sin and the effects of God's law. Read this passage carefully.

a. What does Paul say is the effect of the law, according to verse 7?

b. What dilemma does Paul describe in verses 15-19?

c. Now answer the following question in light of the truths Paul addresses in Romans 7:7-20: To what extent do you think strict laws and appropriate punishments can make people "good," or produce good behavior in them?

8. If one purpose of punishment is to help rehabilitate criminals, what type of punishment do you think is most likely to achieve that goal, and why?

9.   a. Read Romans 8:1-4. According to this passage, what is needed for us to fulfill the requirements of God's law?

b. Consider now the following two issues: (1) society's role in regulating its citizens' behavior and punishing wrongdoing; and (2) the truth that only through inner transformation by the power of God's Spirit can we overcome sin.

Write out a brief paragraph explaining your opinion of how the Christian ought to integrate these two areas in facing the issues of crime and punishment in contemporary society.

10. The death penalty continues to be a major issue in the debate over crime and punishment in our society. In the chart below, summarize what you believe to be the major arguments for and against capital punishment.

Arguments for capital punishment	Arguments against capital punishment

11. Now examine some passages from the Old Testament that deal with the death penalty.

a. In ancient Israel, criminals were not punished by imprisonment, but most often by restitution (we will study restitution in session six). The death penalty, however, was invoked for many offenses. In the following passages, list the offense that called for death.

Exodus 21:12

Exodus 35:2

Leviticus 20:10

Leviticus 20:13

Deuteronomy 17:2-5

b. Do these Old Testament precedents justify the use of capital punishment today? Why or why not?

c. If you do feel that capital punishment is justified today, for what crimes should the death penalty be invoked?

12. a. In order to ensure that the death penalty was adminis-
     tered justly, Old Testament law required certain safeguards.
     According to the following passages, what conditions had to
     be met before a person could be sentenced to death?

Numbers 35:9-12

Numbers 35:29-31

Deuteronomy 24:16

b. In order for the death penalty to be administered justly in
our society, what safeguards do you think are needed?

c. In your opinion, are these conditions being met?

d. If these conditions are not being met, do you think Christians should try to reform our justice system to provide these
safeguards, or should they work to abolish the death
penalty?

13. a. Summarize the incident that John 8:1-11 records in which the enforcement of Jewish law was abruptly interrupted.

b. Should this story of the woman caught in adultery have any bearing on our decisions or attitudes about capital punishment? Why or why not?

14. How do you think Christians who differ about capital punishment can work together to promote justice in our criminal system?

15. Write down any questions you have about issues of crime and punishment and how God's Word speaks to us in this area.

For Further Reflection

As a Christian, I most certainly believe in punishment. Biblical justice demands that individuals be held accountable. Throughout the history of ancient Israel, to break God's laws was to invite swift, specific, and certain punishment. When a law was broken, the resulting imbalance could be righted only when the transgressor was punished, and thus made to "pay" for his wrong.

Though modern sociologists take offense at this elemental concept of retribution, it is essential: If justice means getting one's due, then justice is denied when deserved punishment is not received. And ultimately this undermines one's role as a moral, responsible human being.

Charles Colson in *Jubilee*

The punishment for sins of which the Bible speaks may certainly . . . be termed retribution, provided only that the word is not understood as carrying overtones of revenge, spite or vindictiveness; for there is no antithesis between God's condemnation of sin and his love for the sinner. On the contrary, the one is the obverse of the other, for he can truly be said to "hate" what causes spiritual injury to those whom he loves.

Sir Norman Anderson,
"Criminal Sanctions,"
in *Crime and the Responsible Community*

If we punish people because we believe they have free choice, then we need to understand that there is always the possibility of choosing to change. Christians, who believe in the importance and reality of repentance and conversion, certainly understand this. We cannot give up on anyone. Second, there must be limits to the amount of punishment that we give, and those limits ought to be based on what the person has done, not what we think they may do in the future.

Daniel W. Van Ness,
Crime and Its Victims

The principal method of punishment employed in Western society, at least for the more serious offenses, is imprisonment. The very fact that in public discussion, at least in America, the two terms— "imprisonment" and "punishment"—tend to be used interchangeably suggests how bankrupt our thinking is in this field. If somebody

*breaks the law, society says "send him to prison." Any punishment
other than prison is met with a howl of protest because society
believes the offender has escaped due punishment. Unfortunately,
this is the way people have been conditioned to think.*
> Charles Colson, "Towards an Understanding of
> Imprisonment and Rehabilitation,"
> in *Crime and the Responsible Community*

Moving into Action

Begin by having group members report on their action steps.
Choose from among the following activities. Encourage one
another to continue to "do justice" as part of God's holy nation.

1. Report on the status of capital punishment in your state.
What is the current law? Who are the offenders most likely to be
sentenced to death? How many are currently on Death Row?

2. Learn what you can about crime prevention programs in
your area.

3. Watch especially for articles on prisons and capital
punishment.

Ideas for Group Worship

Issues like capital punishment can be emotionally charged. If any
tensions have developed within your group, pray for mutual
understanding and reconciliation. Read aloud Psalm 103. Pray
for victims of crime. Pray for those awaiting death on Death
Row. Ask God to bless the action steps you plan to take.

Reading Resources

Sir Norman Anderson, "Criminal Sanctions," in *Crime and the
Responsible Community*.

Charles Colson, "Towards an Understanding of the Origins of
Crime," in *Crime and the Responsible Community*, eds. John
Stott and Nicholas Miller (Grand Rapids: Eerdmans Pub-
lishing Co., 1980).

Justice Fellowship, *A Call to Dialogue on Capital Punishment*,
available at no cost from Justice Fellowship, P.O. Box
17181, Washington, DC 20041-0180.

Daniel W. Van Ness, *Crime and Its Victims* (Downers Grove, Ill.:
InterVarsity Press, 1986), esp. "The Purposes of Punishment" and pages 184-191 on capital punishment.

"I Was in Prison . . ."

We visited the segregation unit that afternoon where more than a hundred men were kept in rows of cages separated by narrow walkways. They were permitted to exercise on the walkway only one hour each day.

Every prison makes its own "law." At Stillwater [a maximum security prison at Stillwater, Minnesota], the "law" was unusually tough. Twelve months was the minimum sentence to the segregation cells. If during the 12 months an inmate broke a single rule, the clock went back to zero and the 12 months started running again. To some violators time soon didn't matter; many went berserk.

The air about us this day was filled with screams, moans, obscenities. The guard cautioned us not to walk in front of the cells; the men, he explained, were given to hurling their own excrement at visitors and guards. It was my first experience in a segregation unit; already I knew I could never forget the smells, sounds and sights. I prayed that somehow something would be done about "holes" like this.

The warden allowed Kirk [a young man in prison for ten years for unarmed robbery of $20] to see us off. As I grasped his bony shoulder in farewell, I wondered how this scrawny young man could survive the horror I'd seen and heard.

After we drove away from Stillwater to the airport where I would catch a flight back to Washington, other questions pelted my mind: How many more Kirks were there? How many other states like Minnesota, proudly progressive on most social issues, maintain wretched pits of violence, filth, and despair like this? Many, I was discovering.

Winston Churchill once said that "the mood and temper of the public with regard to the treatment of crime and criminals is one of the most unfailing tests of the civilization of any country." How do we Americans rate?

Poor, I'd say.

No one cares—or do they? Who is going to do something about the thousands of Kirks trapped by circumstance, about the horrid conditions of caged men? Christians ought to be working in places like this.

Like the muffled drumroll of distant artillery, the words of the prophet Amos rumbled in my ears:

Hate evil and love the good;
remodel your courts into true halls of justice.
Perhaps even yet the Lord God of Hosts will have mercy
on his people. . . .

Life Sentence

Opening Reflection

1. What is your response to this description of prison conditions?

2. Have you ever been in a prison? Recall your experience.

3.　a. What is your present attitude toward those in prisons? How has it been formed (from direct experience, movies and TV, books)?

b. Is your attitude changing as a result of this study? If so, in what ways?

Turning to the Scriptures

4. a. What warning does Jesus give in Luke 21:12? (For context, read 21:5-13.)

b. Where today are Christians imprisoned for their faith?

5. The writer of the book of Hebrews was addressing primarily Jewish Christians, in a time of religious persecution.

a. In Hebrews 10:32-34, for what did he commend these believers?

b. In 13:3, what did he instruct them regarding those who had been imprisoned? (Write out the verse.)

c. Why do you think he needed to remind them to do this?

6. a. Based upon the passages in Hebrews you just looked at, what do you think Christians in this country should be doing about or for believers imprisoned for their faith?

b. Should this same concern be extended to all prisoners, regardless of the reason for their imprisonment? Why or why not?

7. a. Compare the passages in Hebrews (of question 5 above) with Matthew 25:31–46. Who does Jesus identify as the prisoners that the "goats" neglected to visit?

b. What does this passage teach about how Christians should respond to those in prison? (Identify the proper motive as well as the right action.)

8.   a. Read Luke 6:27-28, 32-36. What does Jesus command of us in this passage, and what is His reason for why we should respond this way?

b. In what ways is this passage applicable to the treatment of criminals?

9.   a. What do Psalms 68:6 and 146:7 declare about God's treatment of prisoners?

b. The prisoners referred to by the psalmist were most likely Israelites held captive by conquering nations. In what sense(s) is this declaration of God's deliverance true for those imprisoned today?

Review your answers to the questions in this chapter so far, and then use those insights to help you answer questions 10 through 13.

10. Finish the following statement:

"The attitudes and actions that God desires of us toward those in prison are . . ."

11. Have you ever visited anyone in prison? Why or why not?

12. In the chart below, write out your opinions about how prisoners in the United States should and shouldn't be treated.

Appropriate treatment	Inappropriate treatment

13. a. A common assumption about our prison system is that its purpose is to rehabilitate criminals and deter crime. How effective do you think it is in achieving this purpose?

b. What is your thinking about the merits of imprisonment for punishing offenders?

14. Write out any questions or reflections you have at this point in your study of justice.

For Further Reflection

We have developed systems of correction which do not correct. . . . If anyone is tempted to regard humane prison reform as "coddling" criminals, let him visit a prison and talk with inmates and staff. I have visited some of the best and some of the worst prisons and have never seen any signs of "coddling," but I have seen the terrible results of the boredom and frustration of empty hours and pointless existence.

Chief Justice of the Supreme Court
Warren Burger,
quoted in *Crime and the Responsible Community*

Our prisons are certainly not effective. The recidivism rate (the percentage of prisoners who get into trouble again after they are released) is high. The FBI reports that 74 percent of the people released from prison will be rearrested within four years.

Daniel W. Van Ness,
Crime and Its Victims

One of the principal justifications for using prisons is the belief that they deter crime. But statistics show that imprisonment is a questionable deterrent to crime. The United States of America, for example, incarcerates more people as a percentage of population than any other country except the Soviet Union and South Africa. Yet the United States also has the highest crime rate in the Western world.

Within our borders the same disparity shows up: in 15 states where prison capacity increased 56 percent from 1955 to 1975, the increase in reported crime was greater than in 15 other states where prison capacity increased only 4 percent. While it is difficult to draw causal connections, it seems that increased imprisonment and longer prison sentences do not deter crime. Indeed, many informed observers have suggested that instead of deterring crime, our prisons contribute to it. Our experience in prisons supports this assertion.

Justice Fellowship,
Is There a Better Way?

I recalled a speech given recently in a conservative church where at one point I said, "I believe in the literal truth of Scripture and the authority of the Bible." Choruses of "amens" roared through the sanctuary. Later I referred passionately to Christ's words that we are to visit those in prison. The sanctuary was silent.

A friend told me afterwards that next to him was a man who had been taking enthusiastic notes throughout the speech. When I urged visiting the prisons, he wrote somberly on his program, "Colson sounds like a do-gooder."

I wanted to shout at them: "Your argument is with Jesus!" But it didn't matter. If believing the literal truth of His words made me a "do-gooder," so be it.

Charles Colson,
Life Sentence

Moving into Action

Report on and discuss any action steps you have taken since your last meeting. Choose from among the following activities. Remember that you can work individually, in pairs, or as a group.

1. Arrange a visit to a nearby jail or prison. If possible, talk with prisoners, staff, and the chaplain.

2. Invite a prison chaplain, staff member, or former inmate to talk with your group about the prison experience.

3. Report on the work of Prison Fellowship Ministries, P.O. Box 17500, Washington, DC 20041. Tell how Christians can help by corresponding with prisoners, visiting inmates, helping ex-offenders, assisting inmates' families, etc.

4. Read Charles Colson's account of his call to prison ministry in *Life Sentence* (Old Tappan, N.J.: Fleming H. Revell Co., 1979) and report to your group.

5. Investigate prison conditions in your state: How many prisoners are there? Where are they imprisoned? What are conditions like?

6. Investigate the work of Amnesty International, which aids prisoners of conscience throughout the world (Amnesty International USA, 322 Eighth Avenue, New York, NY 10001); or the work of CREED (Christian Rescue Effort for the Emancipation of Dissidents), which is active in iron-curtain countries (CREED, 325 North Pitt Street, Alexandria, VA 22314).

7. Continue to clip articles on imprisonment.

Ideas for Group Worship

Have someone in the group read aloud Matthew 25:31-46. After the reading, take several minutes of silence for reflection. Pray for those in prison, for prison staff, for those who minister in prisons. Pray about the action steps you plan to take. Ask the Lord to show you if there is anything you should do now for "the least of these."

Reading Resources

Charles Colson, *Life Sentence* (Old Tappan, N.J.: Fleming H.
    Revell Co., 1979).
Charles Colson, "Toward an Understanding of Imprisonment
    and Rehabilitation," in *Crime and the Responsible Community*

(Grand Rapids: Eerdmans Publishing Co., 1980).
Daniel W. Van Ness, *Crime and Its Victims* (Downers Grove, Ill.: InterVarsity Press, 1986), esp. "Prisoners" and "Being Imprisoned."

Restitution and Restoration

Recently I met with a group of key legislators to suggest alternatives to a massive prison building program underway in their state. Seldom have I encountered such passion. "We're finally getting crime under control," one assured me. "More people are locked up here than ever before, and the public won't be happy until they're all locked up!" (I wasn't sure who "they all" were.)

Others nodded vigorously. These representatives were obviously well-pleased with the job they were doing for their constituents.

Later, however, I had the opportunity to meet with a group of concerned citizens. An older man shook his fist at me. "The legislature isn't doing anything but building new prisons!" he shouted. "When is this ever going to end?"

I can't say I was unhappy to leave this troubled state. While some politicians were whipping up crime as an emotional campaign issue, most seemed to know better, but believed they were under public pressure.

When I returned home I came across some fascinating reports that reinforced my experiences on my trip. According to several studies, there is wide divergence of opinion between policy-makers and the public when it comes to crime.

A national study concluded that politicians are misguided when they believe that the public has become more "punitive" in recent years—and wrong when they base correctional policy changes on this simplistic assumption.

A Maryland report comparing the opinions of the general public with policymakers' perceptions of public opinion showed that officials overestimate by more than 100 percent public opposition to alternatives to prison. Sadly, the report noted that abandonment of reform efforts in Maryland in the early 1980s was probably due to policymakers' misperception of public opinion.

A Washington state survey discovered that officials perceive the public as an obstacle to correctional reform. But public attitudes were far less punitive than policymakers thought, and far more receptive to correctional reform.

The national study concluded, ". . . few would endorse the practice of policy development that flows reactively from 'poll watching' by public officials. In short, the improper use of public opinion data in policy development has been likened to the manner in which a drunk employs a lamppost: for support rather than illumination."

While such language may be harsh, I believe these reports contain a distressing truth. For years, "lock 'em up and throw away the key" has been a traditional get-tough political cry, guaranteed to play off the fears of one's audience and win support.

Today, as public attitudes appear to have changed, the rhetoric continues, but it is missing its mark. What is tragic is that policymakers don't seem to realize it.

How long can states under court order for overcrowding— 32 in this country today—continue to build new prisons, breaking already over-taxed budgets? Policymakers must wake up soon, and arrive at a point of realistic, redemptive prison alternatives. And when they do, they'll find that much of the public is already there, waiting for them.

The Justice Report

Opening Reflection

1. "We're finally getting crime under control. More people are locked up than ever before, and the public won't be happy until they're all locked up!" What understanding of crime and punishment is revealed by this comment?

2. What are some alternative views to the "lock 'em up and throw away the key" position?

3. In your opinion, how receptive are your community and state to alternatives to building new prisons?

Turning to the Scriptures
4. In Old Testament Israel the common punishment for crime was not imprisonment, but restitution. Briefly summarize the examples of restitution in each of these passages.

Exodus 21:18-19

Exodus 21:22-23

Exodus 21:28-32

Exodus 21:33-34

Exodus 22:5

5.   a. What instructions are the Israelites given about the amount of restitution in each of the following cases?

Exodus 22:1

Exodus 22:4

Exodus 22:5

Leviticus 6:1-17

b. Why do you think the amounts differ?

Note: See "How Much Restitution?" in Van Ness, *Crime and Its Victims* (pages 210-211).

6. Read 2 Samuel 12:1-14, in which the prophet Nathan tells David a story about a guilty man in order to trigger David's recognition and repentance of his sin.

    a. What was David's response to the guilty man in the story? (verses 5-6)

    b. What was the payment that God enacted for David's sin? (verses 10-14)

    c. Do you think restitution was possible in David's case? Why or why not?

    d. Read the rest of the passage—12:15-24. Remember that God had not enforced the customary penalty for adultery: death. Can you find any principles in God's treatment of David that are relevant for contemporary issues of punishment and restitution?

7. a. Read Luke 19:1-9. How is the principle of restitution applied here?

b. What do you think accounts for Zacchaeus' action in verse 8?

8. How might the biblical principle of restitution be applied today in the case of the following crimes?

Tax fraud

Theft

Vandalism

Personal injury

A drunk driver who injures or kills another person

9. a. What do you see as some of the practical difficulties of
    making restitution work today?

    b. How might these difficulties be handled?

10. How might restitution be preferable to imprisonment . . .

for the victim?

for the offender?

11. a. Read Paul's passage on the ministry of reconciliation, in
2 Corinthians 5:17-21. Who is being reconciled?

b. What is the effect of this reconciliation?

c. In what sense is it possible for offenders and victims to be
reconciled?

d. What should be the desired effect of such reconciliation?

e. How could Christians become "ministers of reconciliation" between . . .

a criminal and his or her victim?

an ex-prisoner and the society he or she is re-entering?

12. In Paul's brief letter to Philemon, he encourages a Christian slave owner to accept back his runaway slave, Onesimus. In this letter can you find any clues to how we (Christians) may be able to help ex-prisoners return to society?

13. List any questions you have from your study in this chapter.

14. Take some time now to review your experiences and insights in working through this study. Consider any changes you have noticed in the following areas, and summarize them while they are still fresh:

Your understanding of God

Your attitude toward prisoners or criminals

Your knowledge and awareness of our justice system

Your desire for further involvement in justice-related issues

For Further Reflection

Although God no longer holds us accountable to Himself for the sins He has forgiven, we still are responsible to the human beings we have hurt. After we have taken the steps of repenting and being reconciled to God, we still have the responsibility to the one against whom we have sinned.

This is the step of restitution: making amends, making good for the loss or damage. It is giving back to the rightful owner something that has been taken away.

Evelyn Christenson,
When God Speaks

I so strongly favor the punishment so frequently prescribed in Scripture—restitution. Taking the profit out of crime will be a far more effective deterrent than prison. In this area, in fact, some laws need to be tightened up so the assets of organized crime members and heavy narcotics dealers can be seized at the time of arrest. This is punishment, and it will work.

Charles Colson,
Who Speaks for God?

Reconciliation is more than simply restoring the financial loss for the victim. There is a broken relationship which must be restored as well. The Old Testament recognized that this relationship did not end when the crime ended. In fact, the punishment was mitigated because of this relationship: the injunction against beating a convicted offender more than forty times referred to him as "your brother" (Deuteronomy 25:3). Victims are my sisters and brothers, but so are offenders. My responsibility is to see that the injuries are repaired and relationships restored.

Daniel W. Van Ness,
Crime and Its Victims

A genuinely biblical view of criminal justice provides the basis for reforms which can improve public safety, lead to enormous savings for American taxpayers, and produce far more effective punishments that will indeed do something to curb rising crime rates. In the process, we will discover that the punishment which is both humane and just is also the most effective.

Justice Fellowship,
Is There a Better Way?

Moving into Action

Share what you have been doing in your action steps. See what you can do to help and support one another. Choose from among these activities.

1. Read up on alternatives to imprisonment in *Is There a Better Way?* available from Justice Fellowship, P.O. Box 17181, Washington, DC 20041-0181.

2. Collect newspaper or magazine articles on alternatives to imprisonment, such as community service, restitution, probation, house arrest, etc.

3. Talk to a lawyer or judge to learn what alternatives to imprisonment are used in your area.
Note: Your group will probably want to meet one more time to hear reports on the actions taken. You may also want to summarize what you have learned and decide whether there is some continuing involvement in justice issues that you wish to take—as individuals or as a group. Plan for some closing worship time together.

Your group may wish to continue meeting to study the other guides by Charles Colson about civic responsibility and political action.

Ideas for Group Worship
Pray for all those in the world who are seeking reconciliation between classes and groups. Pray for those who are working for reform of our justice system. Ask God to show you what He wants you to do to "let justice roll down like waters." Close by singing, or reading together, the hymn "Blest Be the Tie That Binds."

Reading Resources
Charles Colson, "Towards an Understanding of Imprisonment and Rehabilitation," in *Crime and the Responsible Community* (Grand Rapids: Eerdmans Publishing Co., 1980).
Justice Fellowship, *Is There a Better Way?* (Washington, D.C.: Justice Fellowship, 1981, 1986).
Daniel W. Van Ness, *Crime and Its Victims* (Downers Grove, Ill.: InterVarsity Press, 1986), esp. "Responding to Crime" and "Restraining Criminals."

Notes

SESSION 1: THE JUSTICE OF GOD
Charles Colson, *Loving God* (Grand Rapids: Zondervan Publishing Co., 1983), pages 128-129.

For Further Reflection
R.C. Sproul, *The Holiness of God* (Wheaton, Ill.: Tyndale House Publishers, 1985), pages 142-143.

Daniel W. Van Ness, *Crime and Its Victims* (Downers Grove, Ill.: InterVarsity Press, 1986), page 114.

A.W. Tozer, *The Knowledge of the Holy* (New York: Harper & Row, 1961), pages 95-96.

Jerry Bridges, *The Pursuit of Holiness* (Colorado Springs, Colo.: NavPress, 1978), pages 25-26.

Charles Colson, *Who Speaks for God?* (Westchester, Ill.: Crossway Books, 1985), pages 36-37.

SESSION 2: THE HOLY NATION
Charles Colson, *Loving God* (Grand Rapids: Zondervan Publishing Co., 1983), pages 175-176.

For Further Reflection
Charles Colson, *Dare to Be Different, Dare to Be Christian* (Wheaton, Ill.: Victor Books/Scripture Press, 1986), page 22.

Clark Pinnock, *A Case for Faith* (Minneapolis: Bethany House, 1980), page 98.

Richard J. Mouw, *Called to Holy Worldliness* (Philadelphia: Fortress Press, 1980), page 43.

Charles Colson, *Kingdoms in Conflict* (Grand Rapids: Zondervan Publishing Co., 1987), page 93.

Charles Colson, *The Struggle for Men's Hearts and Minds* (Wheaton, Ill.: Victor Books/Scripture Press, 1986), page 42.

SESSION 3: DEFENDING THE DEFENSELESS
Charles Colson, *Life Sentence* (Old Tappan, N.J.: Fleming H. Revell Co., 1979), pages 297-298.

For Further Reflection
Charles Colson, *Loving God* (Grand Rapids: Zondervan Publishing Co., 1983), page 145.

Stephen Charles Mott, *Biblical Ethics and Social Change* (New York: Oxford University Press, 1982), page 65.

Charles Colson, *Who Speaks for God?* (Grand Rapids: Zondervan Publishing Co., 1983), page 158.

SESSION 4: CRIME AND PUNISHMENT
Charles Colson, *Who Speaks for God?* (Grand Rapids: Zondervan Publishing Co., 1983), pages 118-119.

For Further Reflection
Charles Colson in *Jubilee* (August 1985), page 7.

Sir Norman Anderson, "Criminal Sanctions," in *Crime and the Responsible Community,* John Stott and Nicholas Miller, eds. (Grand Rapids: Eerdmans Publishing Co., 1980), page 52.

Daniel W. Van Ness, *Crime and Its Victims* (Downers Grove, Ill.: InterVarsity Press, 1986), page 94.

Charles Colson, "Towards an Understanding of Imprisonment and Rehabilitation," in *Crime and the Responsible Community,* page 152.

SESSION 5: "I WAS IN PRISON . . ."
Charles Colson, *Life Sentence* (Old Tappan, N.J.: Fleming H. Revell Co., 1979), pages 56-57.

For Further Reflection
Warren Burger in *Crime and the Responsible Community* (Grand Rapids: Eerdmans Publishing Co., 1980), page 154.

Daniel W. Van Ness, *Crime and Its Victims* (Downers Grove, Ill.: InterVarsity Press, 1986), page 45.

Is There a Better Way? (Washington, D.C.: Justice Fellowship, 1981, 1986), page 7.

Charles Colson, *Life Sentence* (Old Tappan, N.J.: Fleming H. Revell Co., 1979), page 116.

SESSION 6: RESTITUTION AND RESTORATION
The Justice Report (Spring 1986), page 3.

Turning to the Scriptures
Daniel W. Van Ness, *Crime and Its Victims* (Downers Grove, Ill.: InterVarsity Press, 1986), pages 210-211.

For Further Reflection
Evelyn Christenson, *When God Speaks* (Waco, Tex.: Word, Inc., 1986), page 117.

Charles Colson, *Who Speaks for God?* (Westchester, Ill.: Crossway Books, 1985), page 119.

Daniel W. Van Ness, *Crime and Its Victims* (Downers Grove, Ill.: InterVarsity Press, 1986), pages 137-138.

Is There a Better Way? (Washington, D.C.: Justice Fellowship, 1981, 1986), page 23.

Suggested Reading

Bridges, Jerry. *The Pursuit of Holiness*. Colorado Springs, Colo.: NavPress, 1978.

A practical look at the struggle to defeat sin and pursue God's holiness. Stresses both personal choice and God's provision for the means to be holy.

Colson, Charles. *Born Again*. Old Tappan, N.J.: Fleming H. Revell Co., 1976, 1977.

Tells the dramatic story of Charles Colson's involvement in Watergate, his imprisonment, and his conversion to faith in Jesus Christ.

Colson, Charles. *Dare to Be Different, Dare to Be Christian*. Wheaton, Ill.: Victor Books/Scripture Press, 1986.

A brief discussion of "What it Means to Be a Citizen in God's Holy Nation," challenging Christians to radical biblical obedience.

Colson, Charles. *Kingdoms in Conflict*. Grand Rapids: Zondervan Publishing Co., 1987.

An in-depth discussion of how we Christians can live as citizens of the Kingdom of God among the kingdoms of the world, providing a biblical perspective on current issues such as war and peace, the Christian in politics, and the separation of church and state.

Colson, Charles. *Life Sentence*. Old Tappan, N.J.: Fleming H. Revell Co., 1979.

Continues the autobiography begun in *Born Again,* showing how God called Charles Colson into prison ministry.

Colson, Charles. *Loving God*. Grand Rapids: Zondervan Publishing Co., 1983.

Lays the biblical foundation for faith and demonstrates that loving God means a life of committed discipleship.

Colson, Charles. *Presenting Belief in an Age of Unbelief.* Wheaton, Ill.: Victor Books/Scripture Press, 1986.

Helps Christians understand the radical changes in our society and suggests strategies for reaching our skeptical, self-centered world for Christ. Part of the "Challenging the Church" series.

Colson, Charles. *The Role of the Church in Society.* Wheaton, Ill.: Victor Books/Scripture Press, 1986.

Corrects the distorted pictures of the Church that are current today and calls on Christians to be bold witnesses for Christ through words and actions. Part of the "Challenging the Church" series.

Colson, Charles. *The Struggle for Men's Hearts and Minds.* Wheaton, Ill.: Victor Books/Scripture Press, 1986.

Shows how Christians can counter the secular mind-set of our society and win it for Christ. Part of the "Challenging the Church" series.

Colson, Charles. *Who Speaks for God?* Westchester, Ill.: Crossway Books, 1985.

Forty-six short chapters on contemporary life and issues, showing how Christians can confront the world with "real Christianity."

Mouw, Richard J. *Called to Holy Worldliness.* Philadelphia: Fortress Press, 1980.

Develops a biblical base of the ministry of the laity, emphasizing the Christian's responsibility for political and social issues.

Pinnock, Clark. *A Case for Faith.* Minneapolis: Bethany House, 1980.

A defense of the truth claims of the Christian faith, based on five circles of evidence.

Sproul, R.C. *The Holiness of God.* Wheaton, Ill.: Tyndale House, 1985.

Investigates the character of God, especially His holiness, as the basis for the Christian's call to holy living.

Stott, John, and Nicholas Miller, eds. *Crime and the Responsible Community.* Grand Rapids: Eerdmans Publishing Co., 1980.

Six essays from the London Lectures in Contemporary Christianity, including Charles Colson's "Towards an Understanding of the Origins of Crime" and "Towards an

Understanding of Imprisonment and Rehabilitation."
Van Ness, Daniel W. *Crime and Its Victims.* Downers Grove, Ill.:
InterVarsity Press, 1986.

From a biblical perspective, a lawyer and director of
Justice Fellowship examines the criminal justice system and
how it can be reformed to aid victims, prevent crime and
rehabilitate offenders. Includes study questions for individuals and groups and foreword by Charles Colson.
Tozer, A.W. *The Knowledge of the Holy.* New York: Harper &
Row, 1961.

A biblical understanding of God's attributes, stressing
the importance of thinking rightly about God.